Editor in Chief
Ina Massler Levin, M.A.

Editor
Eric Migliaccio

Contributing Editor
Sarah Smith

Creative Director
Karen J. Goldfluss, M.S. Ed.

Cover Design
Tony Carrillo / Marilyn Goldberg

Teacher Created Resources, Inc.
6421 Industry Way
Westminster, CA 92683
www.teachercreated.com

ISBN: 978-1-4206-5977-1

©2007 Teacher Created Resources, Inc.
Reprinted, 2011 (PO4861)
Made in U.S.A.

This book belongs to

_____

Ready·Set·Learn

Get Ready to Learn!

Get ready, get set, and go! Boost your child's learning with this exciting series of books. Geared to help children practice and master many needed skills, the *Ready·Set·Learn* books are bursting with 64 pages of learning fun. Use these books for . . .

 enrichment   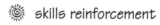 skills reinforcement   extra practice

With their smaller size, the *Ready·Set·Learn* books fit easily in children's hands, backpacks, and book bags. All your child needs to get started are pencils, crayons, and colored pencils.

A full sheet of colorful stickers is included. Use these stickers for . . .

- decorating pages

- rewarding outstanding effort

- keeping track of completed pages

Celebrate your child's progress by using these stickers on the reward chart located on the inside cover. The blue-ribbon sticker fits perfectly on the certificate on page 64.

With *Ready Set Learn* and a little encouragement, your child will be on the fast track to learning fun!

Uppercase Cups

Directions: Fill in the missing uppercase letters.

4

Lowercase Cups

Directions: Fill in the missing lowercase letters.

Erupting Volcano

Directions: Color the big circles red. Color the small circles yellow.

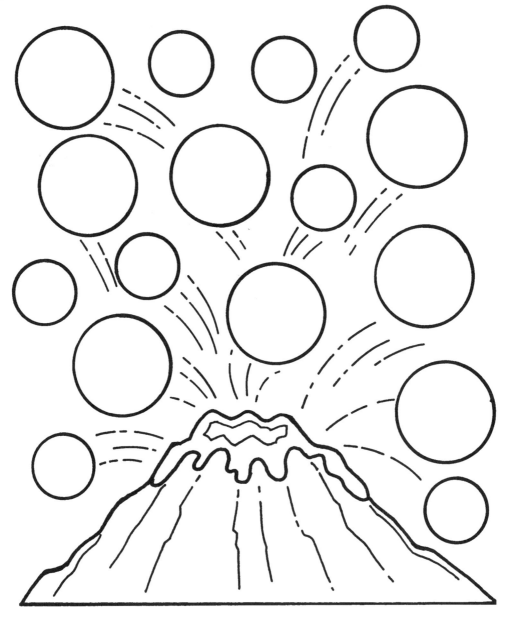

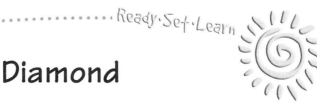

Diamond

Directions: Trace on the dotted line to form the diamond shape within the picture. Draw a picture of an object shaped like a diamond in the space below.

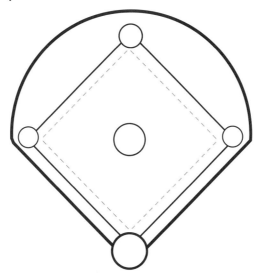

Diamond

What Doesn't Belong?

Directions: Circle the picture in each row that doesn't belong with the others. Color the pictures.

Farm Pattern

Directions: Look at the color words next to each row. Color the animals in that row that color.

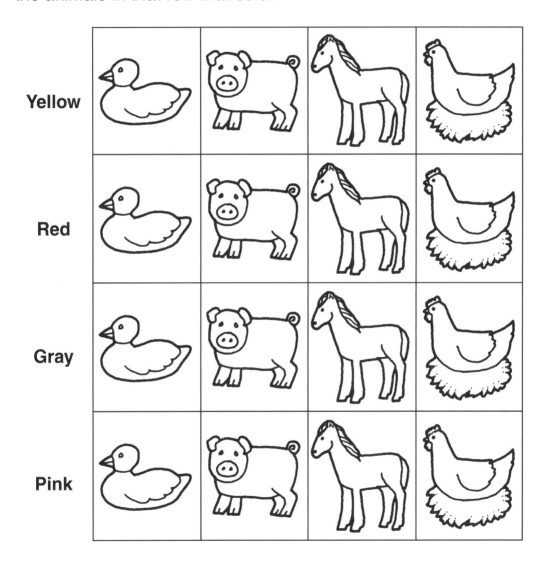

Yellow				
Red				
Gray				
Pink				

Follow the Directions

Directions: Make an **X** inside the acorn. Draw a line under the moon. Color the heart blue. Draw a circle around the fish.

10

How to Draw a Spider

Directions: Follow the directions in each box and draw a spider.

1. Make the spider's head.	**2.** Add a face.
3. Add a body.	**4.** Add spinnerets.
5. Add four legs to one side.	**6.** Add four more legs.

Draw your spider here.

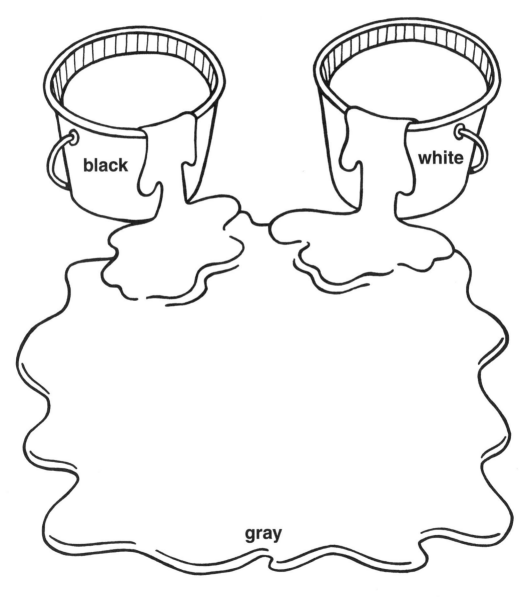

Mixing Up Colors

Directions: What happens when you mix black and white? Color the cans and find out. First, color each can the color it says, then color the paint with black and white.

black

white

gray

12

Find the Pairs

Directions: Be a detective! Color the magnifying glasses that have matching uppercase and lowercase letters.

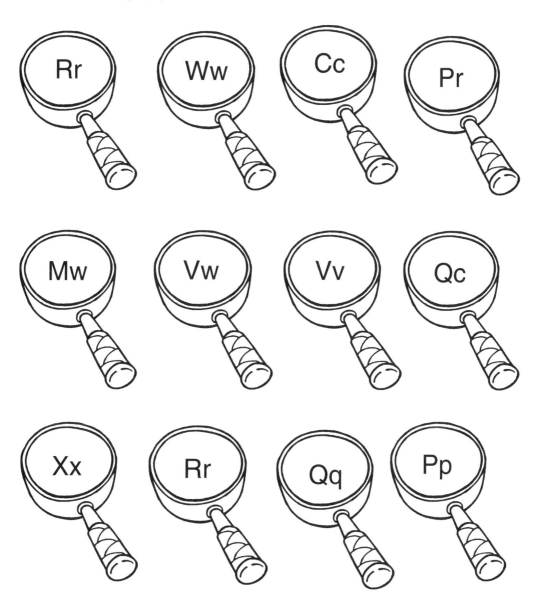

Follow the Directions

Directions: Draw a line from the flower to the bunny. Circle the clock. Color the sun yellow.

14

How to Draw a Pumpkin

Directions: Follow the directions in each box to draw a pumpkin.

1. Draw a half-circle. 	**2.** Draw another half-circle. 
3. Draw a stem. 	**4.** Add lines to shape the pumpkin. 

Draw your pumpkin here.

Red, Orange, and Gold

Directions: Connect the dots from 1 to 10 to discover what fell off the tree. Color your picture.

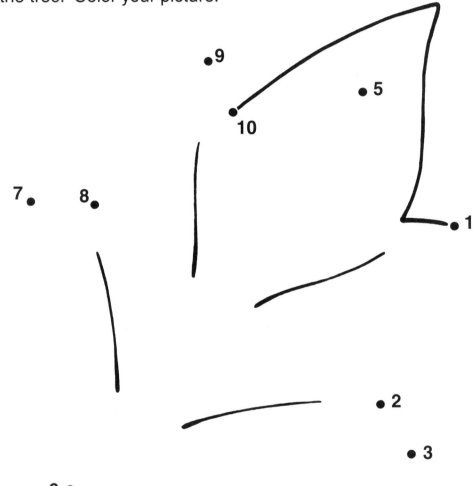

What's Missing?

Directions: Draw what's missing on the second animal in each row. Color the pictures.

Hot and Cold

Directions: Look at each picture. Use a red crayon to color the items that could be hot. Use a blue crayon to color the items that could be cold.

18

All in the Family

Directions: Find and circle each word.

```
G  R  A  N  D  M  A  A  B  C
F  A  T  H  E  R  Q  Z  R  D
U  N  C  L  E  Y  A  U  N  T
M  O  T  H  E  R  J  K  A  E
N  N  I  E  C  E  T  X  S  F
M  B  I  H  S  I  S  T  E  R
L  C  U  G  R  A  N  D  P  A
N  E  P  H  E  W  W  F  G  G
B  A  B  Y  C  O  U  S  I  N
J  I  B  R  O  T  H  E  R  H
```

AUNT	FATHER	NEPHEW
BABY	GRANDMA	NIECE
BROTHER	GRANDPA	SISTER
COUSIN	MOTHER	UNCLE

Heart Patterns

Directions: Color the hearts to create a pattern for each row.

Real and Make-Believe

Directions: Put a line under the animals that are real. Draw a circle around the animals that are make-believe.

Finish the Animals

Directions: Draw the missing parts on the second animal in each row. Color the pictures.

22

Rectangle

Directions: Trace on the dotted lines to form the rectangle shapes within the picture. Draw a picture of an object shaped like a rectangle in the space below.

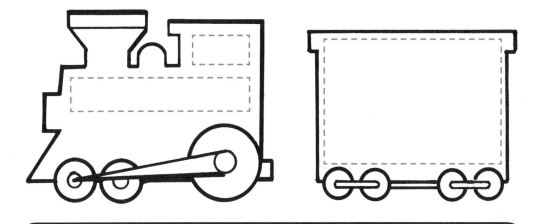

Rectangle

Complete the Animal

Directions: Draw the missing parts on the second animal in each row. Color the animals.

Identify Vowel Pairs

Directions: Which way should you go? Color the signs with the matching pairs.

Tiny Raindrops

Directions: Connect the raindrops from 1–15 to find the picture. Color the picture.

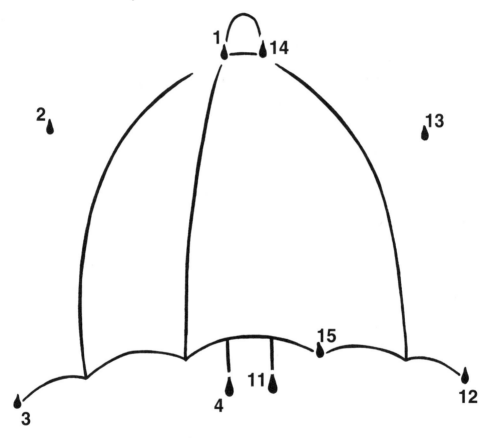

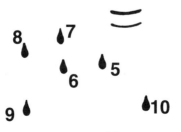

Sorting Buttons

Directions: Follow the directions to color the buttons.

Color these red.	Color these orange.	Color these blue.	Color these purple.

Long Vowels

Directions: Say the name of each picture. Circle the letter that makes the long vowel sound within each word.

1.	2.	3.
a e i o u	a e i o u	a e i o u

4.	5.	6.
a e i o u	a e i o u	a e i o u

7.	8.	9.
a e i o u	a e i o u	a e i o u

What Comes Next?

Directions: Find the pattern in each row. Draw the shape that comes next.

1.

 _____

2.

    _____

3.

    _____

4.

  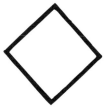 _____

5.

    _____

What Doesn't Belong?

Directions: Circle the picture that doesn't belong with the others. Color the pictures.

Clean Clothes

Directions: Color the clothes inside the laundry basket *orange*. Color the clothes outside the laundry basket *green*.

An "E" Puzzle

Directions: Say the name of each picture. Find and circle the matching word in the puzzle below.

head	tent	pets	leg

pen	hen	elf	elephant

e	l	e	p	h	a	n	t
l	h	t	e	n	t	e	e
f	e	e	t	h	e	a	d
w	e	t	s	e	l	e	g
e	p	e	n	e	h	e	n

How to Draw a Kitten

Directions: Follow the directions in each box and draw a kitten.

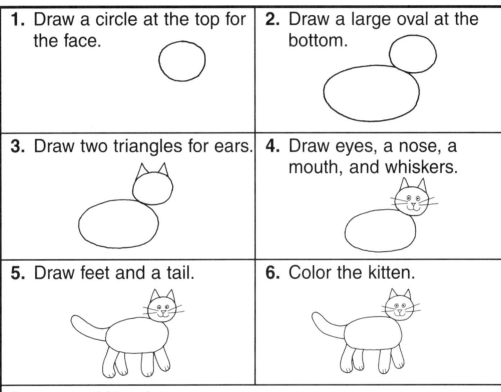

1. Draw a circle at the top for the face.

2. Draw a large oval at the bottom.

3. Draw two triangles for ears.

4. Draw eyes, a nose, a mouth, and whiskers.

5. Draw feet and a tail.

6. Color the kitten.

Draw your kitten here.

Which Bowl Has More?

Directions: Look at each of the pet's bowls. Circle each animal's bowl that has the most food.

34

Rabbit Numbers

Directions: How many rabbits can you count in each group?
Color 10 of the rabbits.

Long Vowel Review

Directions: Blend the sounds together to say each word. Circle the correct picture.

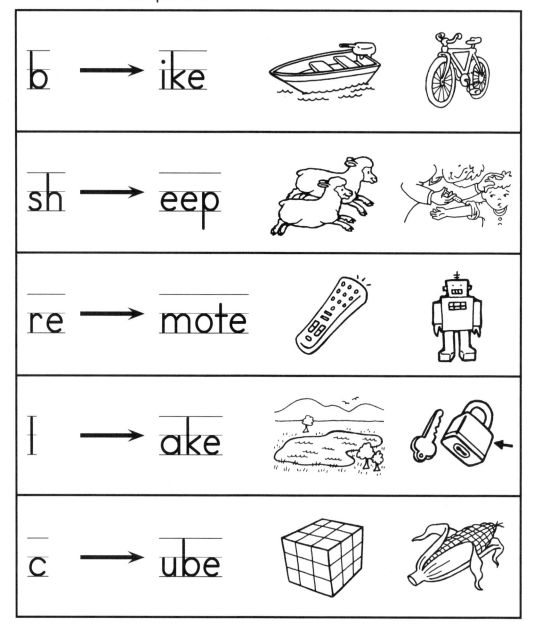

b → ike

sh → eep

re → mote

l → ake

c → ube

Red and Yellow

Directions: Color the paint coming from the bucket on the left *red*. Color the paint coming from the bucket on the right *yellow*. Color the spilled paint at the bottom *orange*.

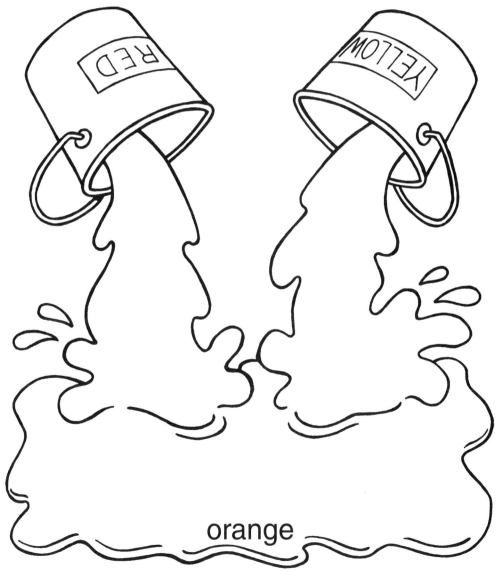

orange

Pretty Flowers

Directions: Color each flower a different color. Use red, blue, pink, yellow, purple, and orange. Color the leaves and stems green.

38

Apple Word Search

Directions: Find and circle each word in the word search.

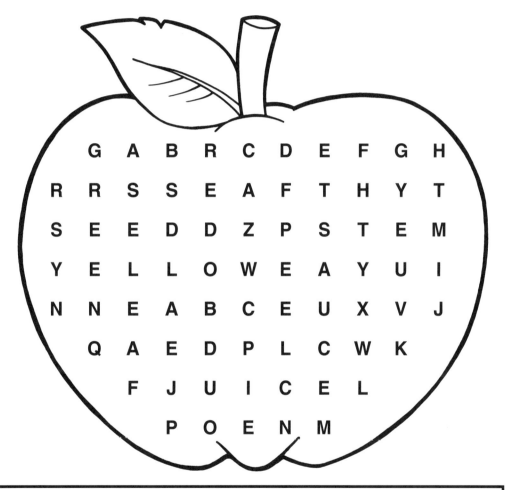

```
G  A  B  R  C  D  E  F  G  H
R  R  S  S  E  A  F  T  H  Y  T
S  E  E  D  D  Z  P  S  T  E  M
Y  E  L  L  O  W  E  A  Y  U  I
N  N  E  A  B  C  E  U  X  V  J
   Q  A  E  D  P  L  C  W  K
   F  J  U  I  C  E  L
      P  O  E  N  M
```

GREEN	PIE	SEED
JUICE	RED	STEM
LEAF	SAUCE	YELLOW
PEEL		

Something Is Missing?

Directions: Draw the missing parts. Color the pictures.

40

Look Who Is Reading!

Directions: Connect the dots from A to Z. Color the picture.

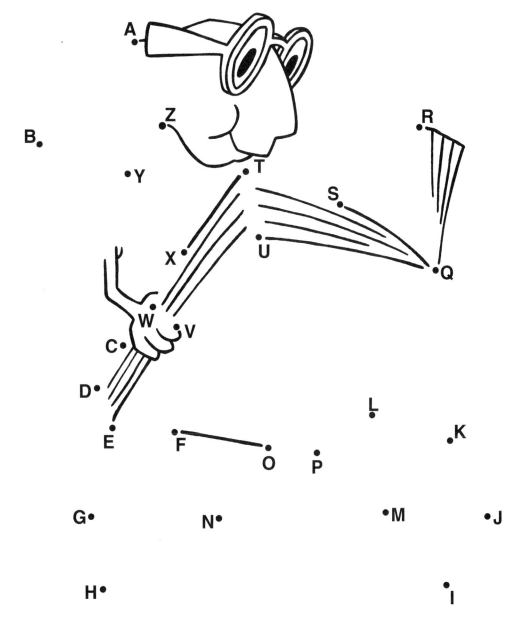

Springtime

Directions: Draw a sun *above* the bird. Draw a flower *between* the trees. Draw a worm *under* the ground. Color the picture.

42

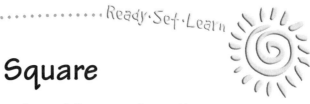

Square

Directions: Trace on the dotted lines to form the square shapes within the picture. Draw a picture of an object shaped like a square in the space below.

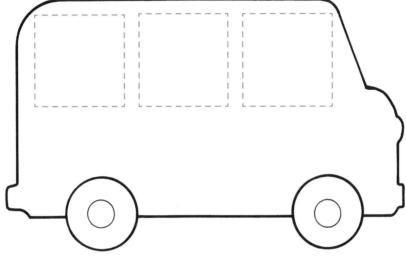

Square

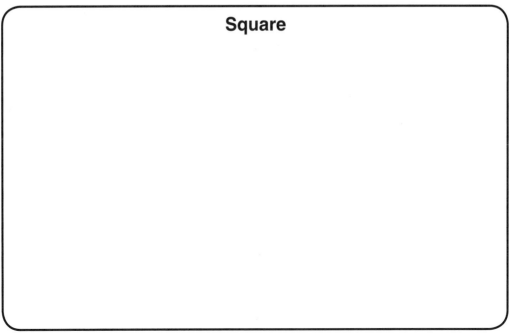

Short Vowels

Directions: Look at the vowel in the first column. Say each picture name in that row. Circle each picture that contains the short vowel sound.

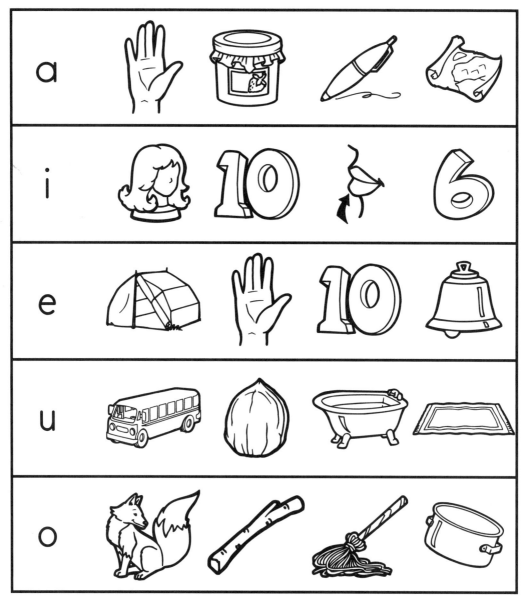

Eggs in a Nest

Directions: The nest is missing its eggs. The tree is missing its leaves. Draw the eggs and leaves.

Rainy Patterns

Directions: Color the raindrops to make a pattern.

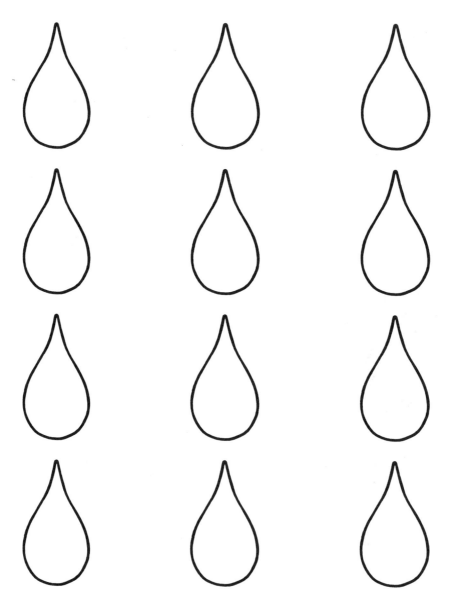

Outside Fun

Directions: Inside the sun, draw two or more things you can do when you play outside.

Garden Snake

Directions: Make a pattern by coloring the spots and lines on the snake. Color the body green.

48

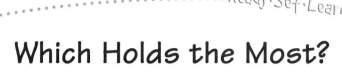

Which Holds the Most?

Directions: Look at each container. Color the container in each row that would hold the most.

Snack Foods

Directions: Read each snack food listed and decide if it is good for you or not good for you. Then put a smile or a frown on the face beside the name of the food.

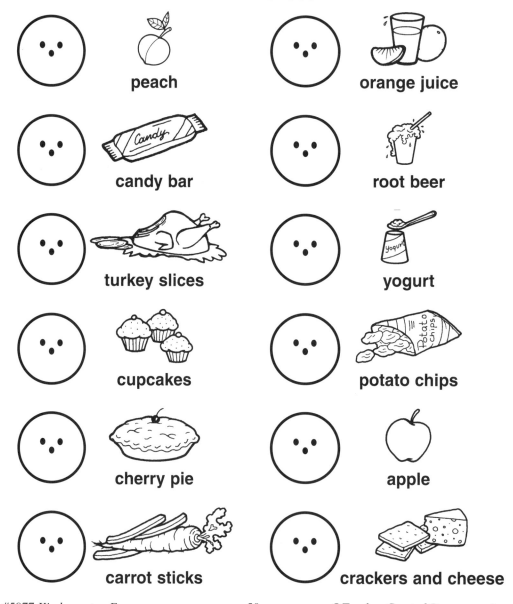

peach

orange juice

candy bar

root beer

turkey slices

yogurt

cupcakes

potato chips

cherry pie

apple

carrot sticks

crackers and cheese

What's Missing?

Directions: Draw the missing parts. Color the pictures.

Our Feathered Friends

Directions: Connect the dots from 1 to 20 to find the picture. Color the picture.

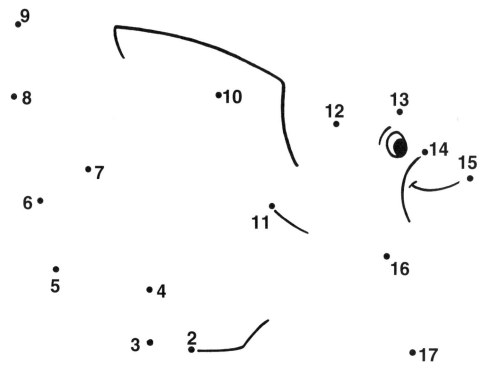

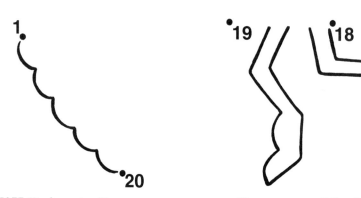

52

Short Vowel Review

Directions: Draw a line from the picture to the letter that matches the short vowel sound.

1.	2.	3.
a e i o u	a e i o u	a e i o u

4.	5.	6.
a e i o u	a e i o u	a e i o u

7.	8.	9.
a e i o u	a e i o u	a e i o u

53   *#5977 Kindergarten Fun*

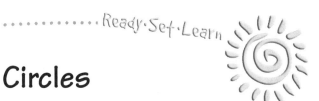

Circles

Directions: Trace on the dotted lines to form the circle shapes within the picture. Draw a picture of an object shaped like a circle in the space below.

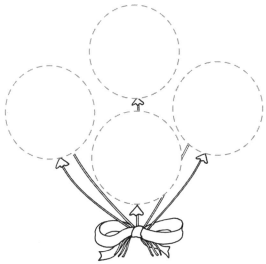

Circle

What are the Animals Missing?

Directions: Draw the missing parts. Color the pictures.

Playing Indoors

Directions: Inside the house, draw two or more things you can do when you play inside.

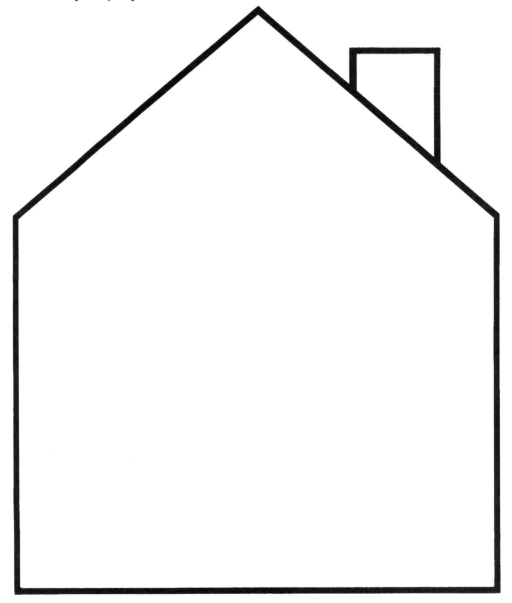

56

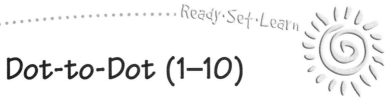

Dot-to-Dot (1–10)

Directions: Follow the numbers to find the picture.

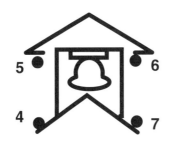

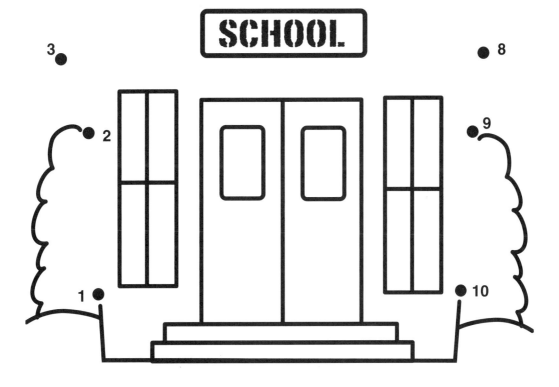

How to Draw a Lamb

Directions: Follow the directions in each box and draw a lamb.

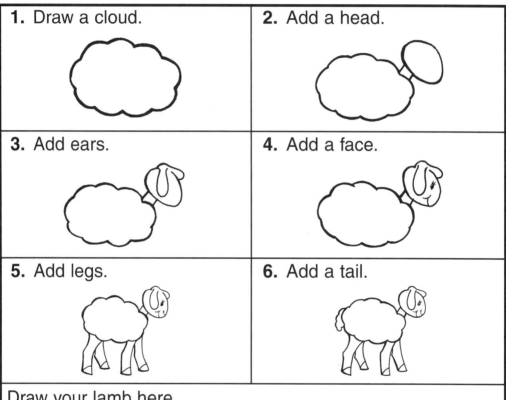

1. Draw a cloud.	**2.** Add a head.
3. Add ears.	**4.** Add a face.
5. Add legs.	**6.** Add a tail.

Draw your lamb here.

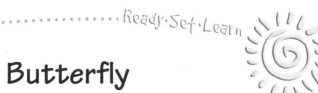

Butterfly

Directions: Color the butterfly.

1–purple	2–yellow	3–orange	4–green

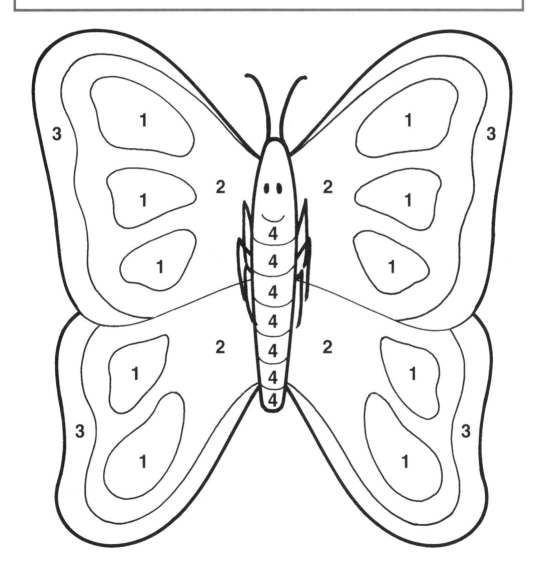

Shapes

Directions: Color the outside of each shape. Draw the shape inside.

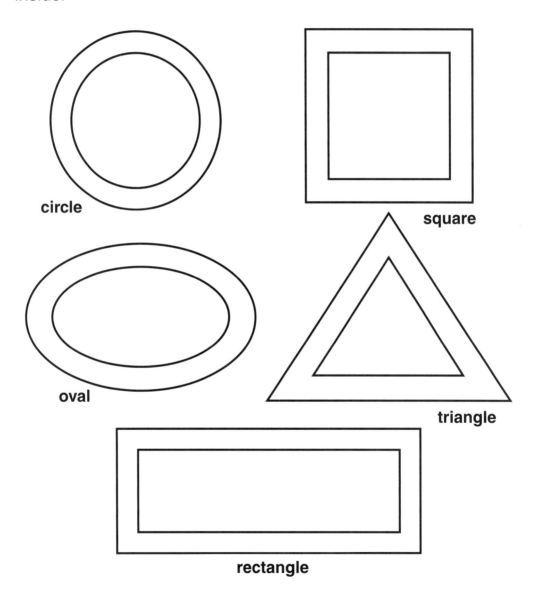

circle

square

oval

triangle

rectangle

Shape Patterns

Directions: Choose two colors. Color each side of each shape a different color.

Bug Sets

Directions: Count the bugs. Write the number in each box.

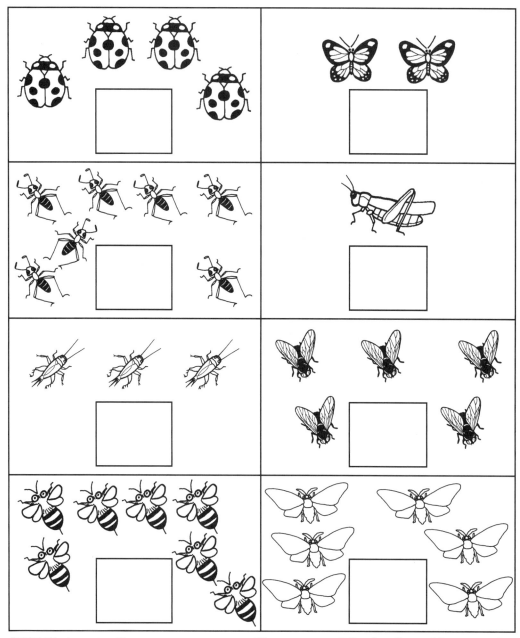

This Award
Is Presented To

_____

for

★ Doing Your Best

★ Trying Hard

★ Not Giving Up

★ Making a
   Great Effort